Revise for Success: Strategies for GCSE Mathematics

Strategy 1: Entrance Tickets

James Rimmer

Publisher's Note

This is the first book in a series of revision resources from James Rimmer and Tarquin. We have made them available in a number of ways - electronically and on paper.

For the full list of titles in the series see below.

For full contents on each title - see www.tarquingroup.com

The Revise for Success series and their book ISBNs

To find a particular resource to meet your need - try www.tarquinselect.com and search by topic and/or age. All the Revise for Success worksheets are there - and hundreds of others besides.

Published by Tarquin Publications
Suite 74, 17 Holywell Hill
St Albans
AL1 1DT, UK
www.tarquingroup.com

© 2018 James Rimmer
ISBN: 978-1-911093-80-0 Book
Printed and bound by CPI Group (UK) Ltd, Croydon, CR0 4YY

How to Use Entrance Tickets

Revise for Success Entrance Tickets provides you with all you need to inspire students to revise in **interesting, active and engaging ways**.

Used as lesson starters, homework tasks or as part of a structured revision session, each A4-size activity sheet will successfully challenge pupils learning on each of the main key strands of the new Mathematics GCSE curriculum focusing on the key skills of **fluency, reasoning and problem solving**.

Executed skilfully, each activity can successfully **engage, excite and energise** students on a daily basis or in the run up to that all-important exam. Designed with busy teachers in mind, the activities are ready-to-go and come with all the answers included. These resources not only perfectly meet the needs of the modern mathematicss teacher, but also those of the dedicated and supportive parent at home. Packed with visual appeal, these activities will enthuse even the most reluctant pupils, and convince them once and for all, that revision can be **enjoyable, rewarding and fun**.

Looking for ways to hook your students as soon as they enter your lesson? Maybe you want to challenge them right from the off? Or perhaps you want to simply include regular revision tasks into your weekly planning? Then look no further. This book *Revise for Success: Entrance Tickets* is a perfect choice.

Instructions:
Each A4 activity sheet has 3 identical tickets ready to photocopy/print then cut to size. They can be handed to students as they enter the class or placed on the student's desk. This activity is a perfect class settler and revision task. It has been designed to improve a student's recall and problem solving skills.

Areas covered: Algebra, Number, Ratio and Proportion, Geometry and Dhape and Statistical Data.

Possible uses: starter task, homework task, revision session.

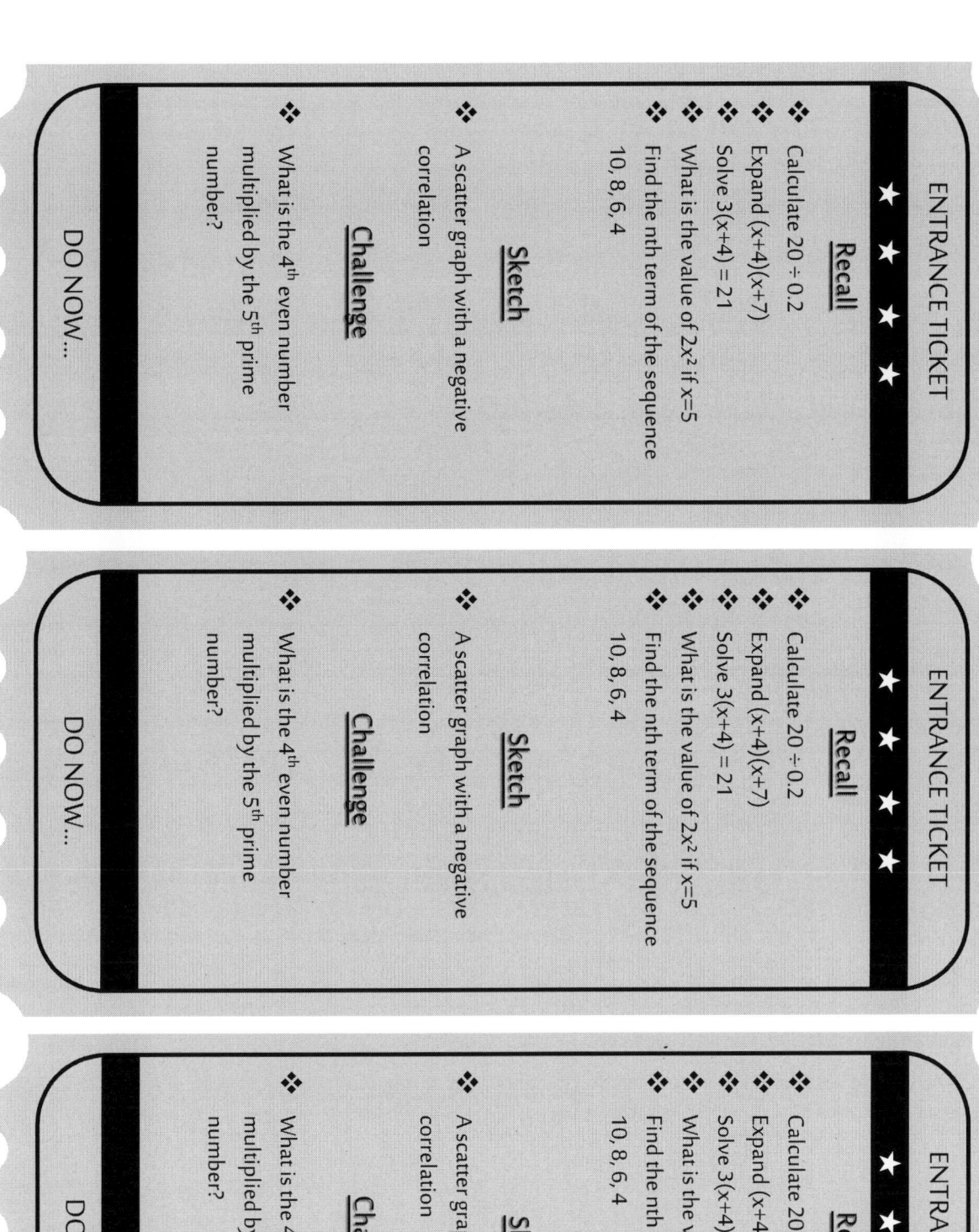

ENTRANCE TICKET ★ ★ ★ ★

Recall

❖ Calculate $20 \div 0.2$
❖ Expand $(x+4)(x+7)$
❖ Solve $3(x+4) = 21$
❖ What is the value of $2x^2$ if $x=5$
❖ Find the nth term of the sequence 10, 8, 6, 4

Sketch

❖ A scatter graph with a negative correlation

Challenge

❖ What is the 4th even number multiplied by the 5th prime number?

DO NOW…

ENTRANCE TICKET ★ ★ ★ ★

Recall

❖ Calculate $20 \div 0.2$
❖ Expand $(x+4)(x+7)$
❖ Solve $3(x+4) = 21$
❖ What is the value of $2x^2$ if $x=5$
❖ Find the nth term of the sequence 10, 8, 6, 4

Sketch

❖ A scatter graph with a negative correlation

Challenge

❖ What is the 4th even number multiplied by the 5th prime number?

DO NOW…

ENTRANCE TICKET ★ ★ ★ ★

Recall

❖ Calculate $20 \div 0.2$
❖ Expand $(x+4)(x+7)$
❖ Solve $3(x+4) = 21$
❖ What is the value of $2x^2$ if $x=5$
❖ Find the nth term of the sequence 10, 8, 6, 4

Sketch

❖ A scatter graph with a negative correlation

Challenge

❖ What is the 4th even number multiplied by the 5th prime number?

DO NOW…

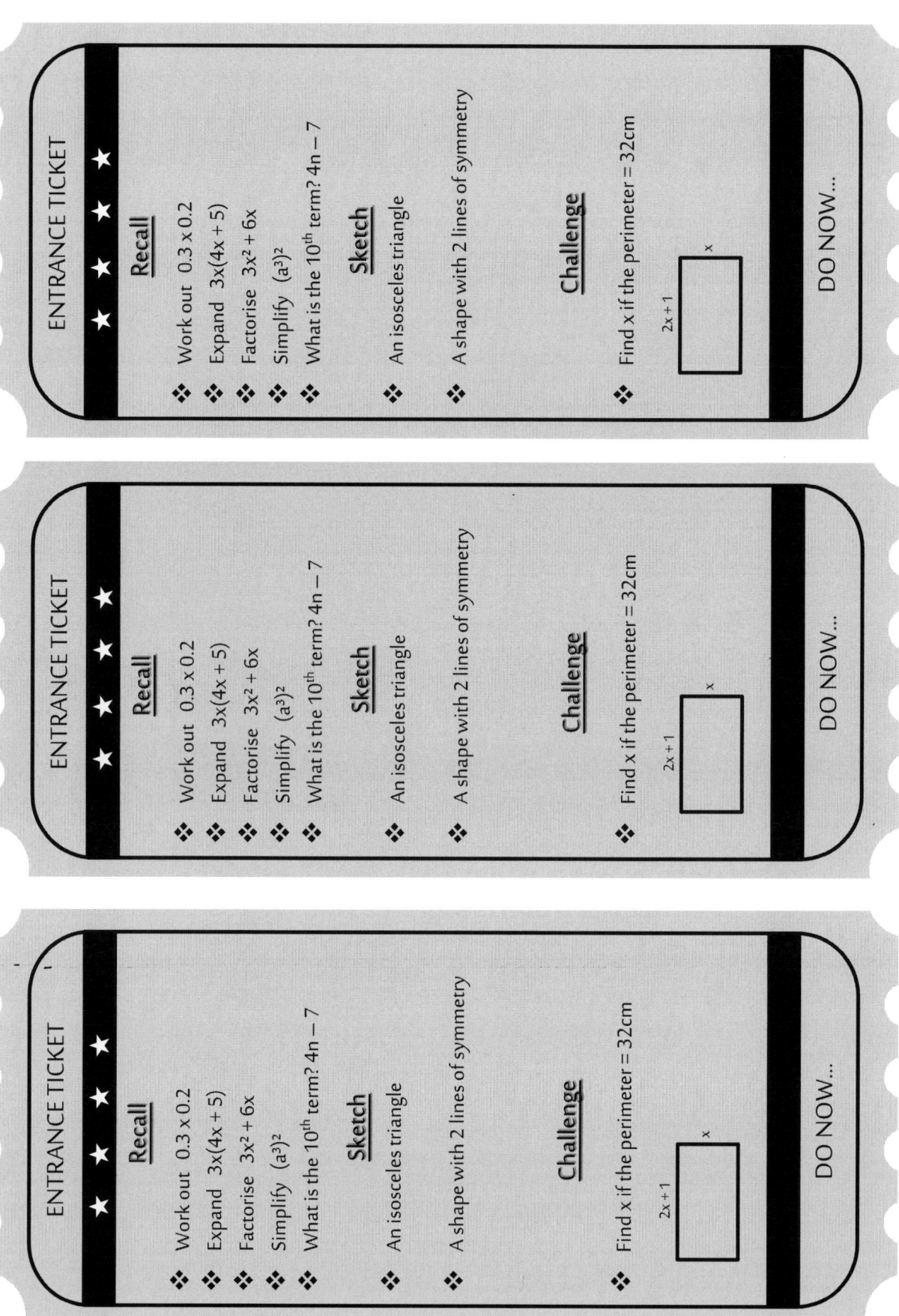

ENTRANCE TICKET ★ ★ ★ ★

Recall

❖ Work out 0.3 x 0.2
❖ Expand 3x(4x + 5)
❖ Factorise 3x² + 6x
❖ Simplify (a³)²
❖ What is the 10ᵗʰ term? 4n − 7

Sketch

❖ An isosceles triangle

❖ A shape with 2 lines of symmetry

Challenge

❖ Find x if the perimeter = 32cm

2x + 1

x

DO NOW...

ENTRANCE TICKET ★ ★ ★ ★

Recall

❖ Work out 0.3 x 0.2
❖ Expand 3x(4x + 5)
❖ Factorise 3x² + 6x
❖ Simplify (a³)²
❖ What is the 10ᵗʰ term? 4n − 7

Sketch

❖ An isosceles triangle

❖ A shape with 2 lines of symmetry

Challenge

❖ Find x if the perimeter = 32cm

2x + 1

x

DO NOW...

ENTRANCE TICKET ★ ★ ★ ★

Recall

❖ Work out 0.3 x 0.2
❖ Expand 3x(4x + 5)
❖ Factorise 3x² + 6x
❖ Simplify (a³)²
❖ What is the 10ᵗʰ term? 4n − 7

Sketch

❖ An isosceles triangle

❖ A shape with 2 lines of symmetry

Challenge

❖ Find x if the perimeter = 32cm

2x + 1

x

DO NOW...

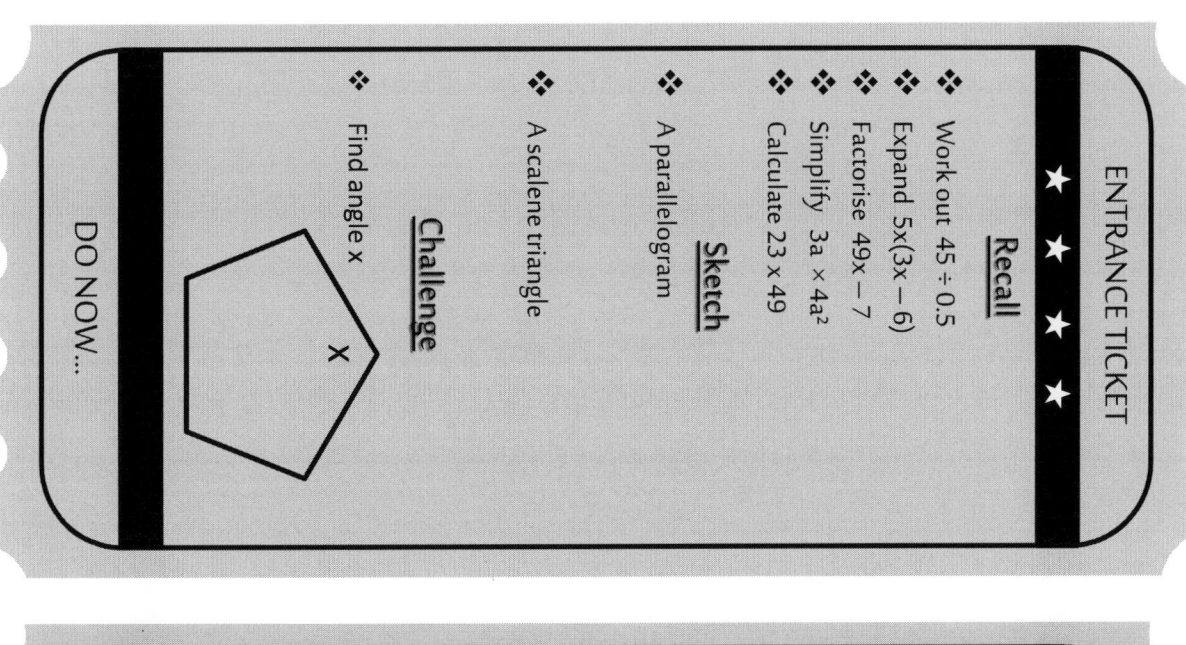

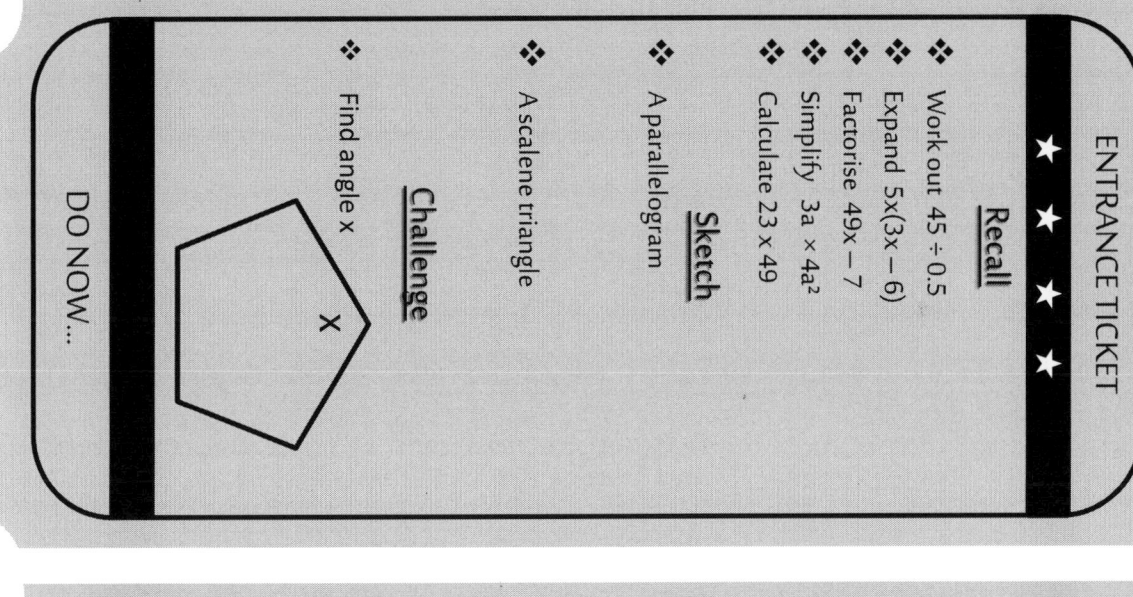

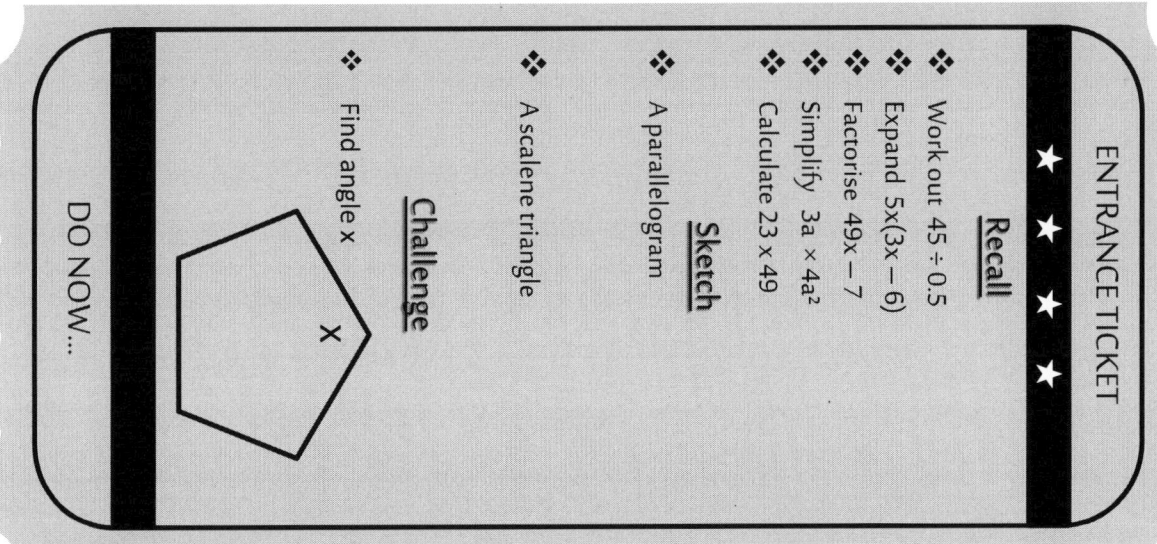

Each entrance ticket contains:

ENTRANCE TICKET

Recall

❖ Work out 45 ÷ 0.5
❖ Expand 5x(3x − 6)
❖ Factorise 49x − 7
❖ Simplify 3a × 4a²
❖ Calculate 23 × 49

Sketch

❖ A parallelogram
❖ A scalene triangle

Challenge

❖ Find angle x

DO NOW...

ISBN 978-1-911093-80-0

ENTRANCE TICKET ★ ★ ★ ★

Recall

❖ Share £300 in ratio 4:1

❖ Expand (x+4)(x-5)

❖ Simplify 3 x b x a x 2 x a

❖ Calculate 45 x 73

❖ Write 160 as a product of its prime factors

Explain

❖ What is meant by a random sample

Challenge

❖ If the mean = 5, find x

3, 7, 5, 4, x

DO NOW...

ENTRANCE TICKET ★ ★ ★ ★

Recall

❖ Share £300 in ratio 4:1

❖ Expand (x+4)(x-5)

❖ Simplify 3 x b x a x 2 x a

❖ Calculate 45 x 73

❖ Write 160 as a product of its prime factors

Explain

❖ What is meant by a random sample

Challenge

❖ If the mean = 5, find x

3, 7, 5, 4, x

DO NOW...

ENTRANCE TICKET ★ ★ ★ ★

Recall

❖ Share £300 in ratio 4:1

❖ Expand (x+4)(x-5)

❖ Simplify 3 x b x a x 2 x a

❖ Calculate 45 x 73

❖ Write 160 as a product of its prime factors

Explain

❖ What is meant by a random sample

Challenge

❖ If the mean = 5, find x

3, 7, 5, 4, x

DO NOW...

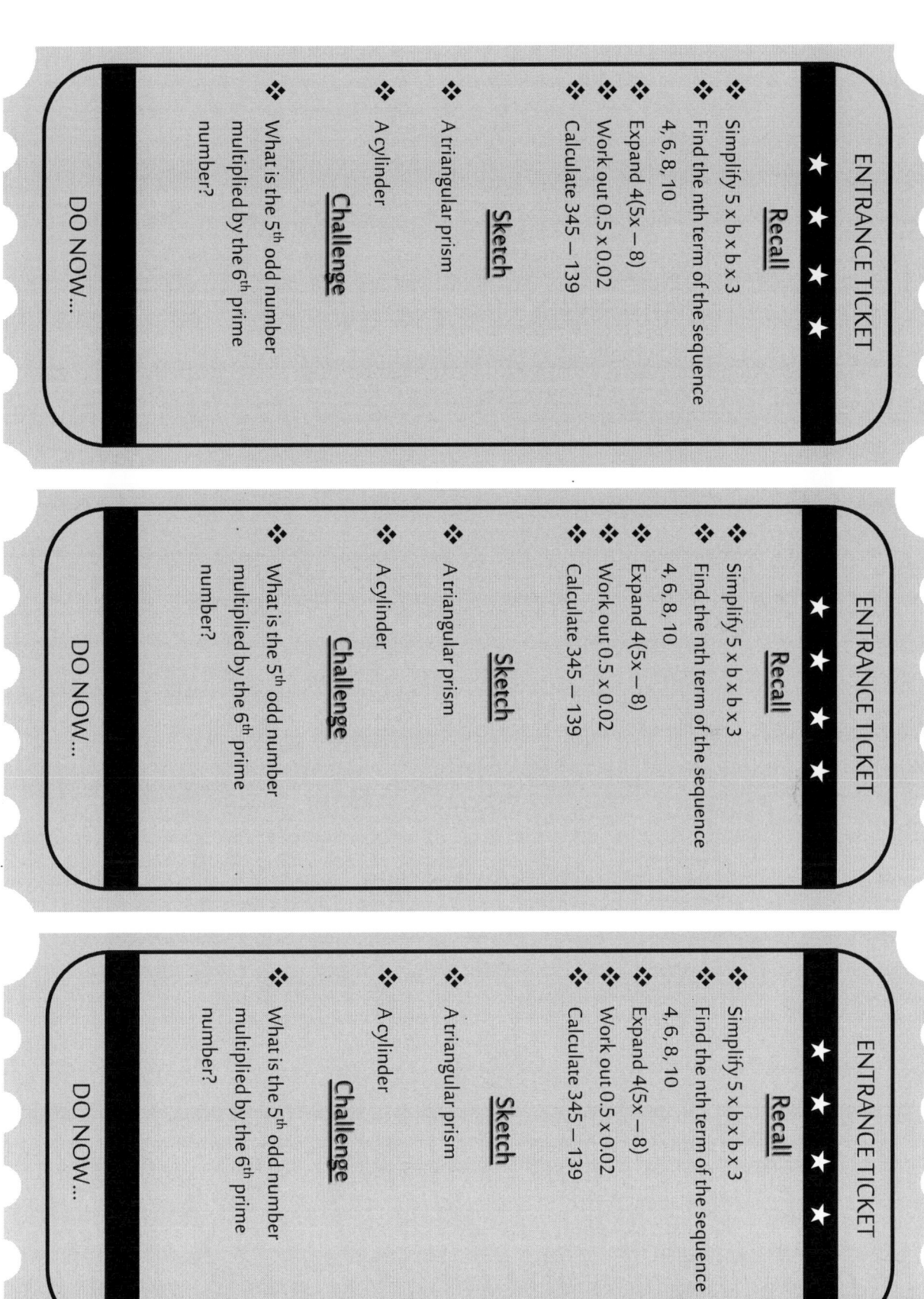

ENTRANCE TICKET ★ ★ ★ ★

Recall

- ❖ Simplify 5 × b × b × 3
- ❖ Find the nth term of the sequence 4, 6, 8, 10
- ❖ Expand 4(5x − 8)
- ❖ Work out 0.5 × 0.02
- ❖ Calculate 345 − 139

Sketch

- ❖ A triangular prism
- ❖ A cylinder

Challenge

- ❖ What is the 5th odd number multiplied by the 6th prime number?

DO NOW...

ENTRANCE TICKET ★ ★ ★ ★

Recall

- ❖ Simplify 5 × b × b × 3
- ❖ Find the nth term of the sequence 4, 6, 8, 10
- ❖ Expand 4(5x − 8)
- ❖ Work out 0.5 × 0.02
- ❖ Calculate 345 − 139

Sketch

- ❖ A triangular prism
- ❖ A cylinder

Challenge

- ❖ What is the 5th odd number multiplied by the 6th prime number?

DO NOW...

ENTRANCE TICKET ★ ★ ★ ★

Recall

- ❖ Simplify 5 × b × b × 3
- ❖ Find the nth term of the sequence 4, 6, 8, 10
- ❖ Expand 4(5x − 8)
- ❖ Work out 0.5 × 0.02
- ❖ Calculate 345 − 139

Sketch

- ❖ A triangular prism
- ❖ A cylinder

Challenge

- ❖ What is the 5th odd number multiplied by the 6th prime number?

DO NOW...

ISBN 978-1-911093-80-0

ENTRANCE TICKET ★ ★ ★ ★

Recall

❖ Share £600 in ratio 4:5:1
❖ Expand $(x+2)(x-6)$
❖ Simplify $a^3 \div a^2$
❖ Calculate $672 \div 12$
❖ Write 120 as a product of its prime factors

Draw

❖ A rectangle with an area of 30cm^2 and a perimeter of 22cm

Challenge

❖ If the mean = 7, find x

3, 12, 8, 4, x

DO NOW...

ENTRANCE TICKET ★ ★ ★ ★

Recall

❖ Share £600 in ratio 4:5:1
❖ Expand $(x+2)(x-6)$
❖ Simplify $a^3 \div a^2$
❖ Calculate $672 \div 12$
❖ Write 120 as a product of its prime factors

Draw

❖ A rectangle with an area of 30cm^2 and a perimeter of 22cm

Challenge

❖ If the mean = 7, find x

3, 12, 8, 4, x

DO NOW...

ENTRANCE TICKET ★ ★ ★ ★

Recall

❖ Share £600 in ratio 4:5:1
❖ Expand $(x+2)(x-6)$
❖ Simplify $a^3 \div a^2$
❖ Calculate $672 \div 12$
❖ Write 120 as a product of its prime factors

Draw

❖ A rectangle with an area of 30cm^2 and a perimeter of 22cm

Challenge

❖ If the mean = 7, find x

3, 12, 8, 4, x

DO NOW...

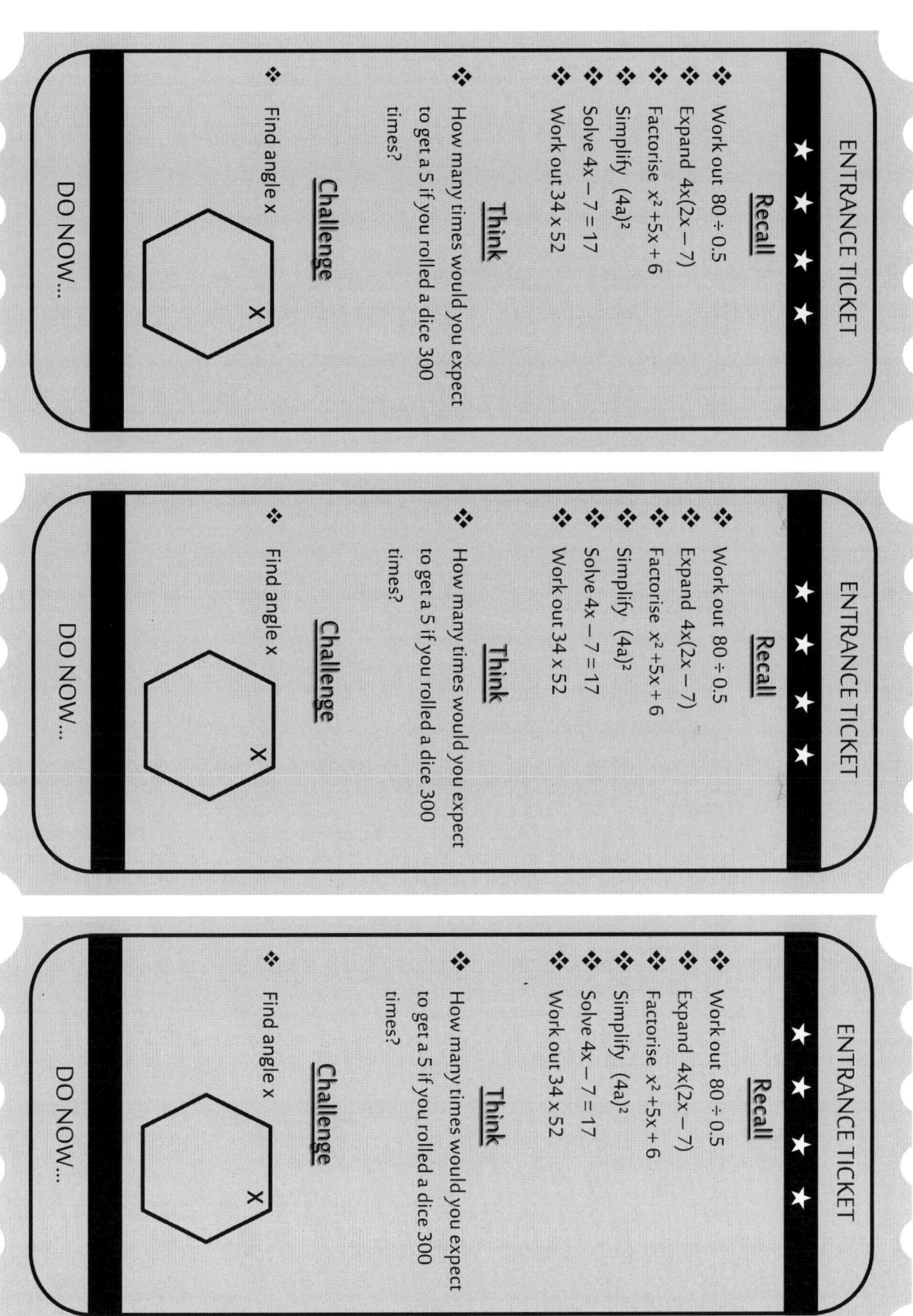

ENTRANCE TICKET

★ ★ ★ ★

Recall

❖ Work out $80 \div 0.5$

❖ Expand $4x(2x - 7)$

❖ Factorise $x^2 + 5x + 6$

❖ Simplify $(4a)^2$

❖ Solve $4x - 7 = 17$

❖ Work out 34×52

Think

❖ How many times would you expect to get a 5 if you rolled a dice 300 times?

Challenge

❖ Find angle x

DO NOW...

ENTRANCE TICKET

★ ★ ★ ★

Recall

❖ Work out $80 \div 0.5$

❖ Expand $4x(2x - 7)$

❖ Factorise $x^2 + 5x + 6$

❖ Simplify $(4a)^2$

❖ Solve $4x - 7 = 17$

❖ Work out 34×52

Think

❖ How many times would you expect to get a 5 if you rolled a dice 300 times?

Challenge

❖ Find angle x

DO NOW...

ENTRANCE TICKET

★ ★ ★ ★

Recall

❖ Work out $80 \div 0.5$

❖ Expand $4x(2x - 7)$

❖ Factorise $x^2 + 5x + 6$

❖ Simplify $(4a)^2$

❖ Solve $4x - 7 = 17$

❖ Work out 34×52

Think

❖ How many times would you expect to get a 5 if you rolled a dice 300 times?

Challenge

❖ Find angle x

DO NOW...

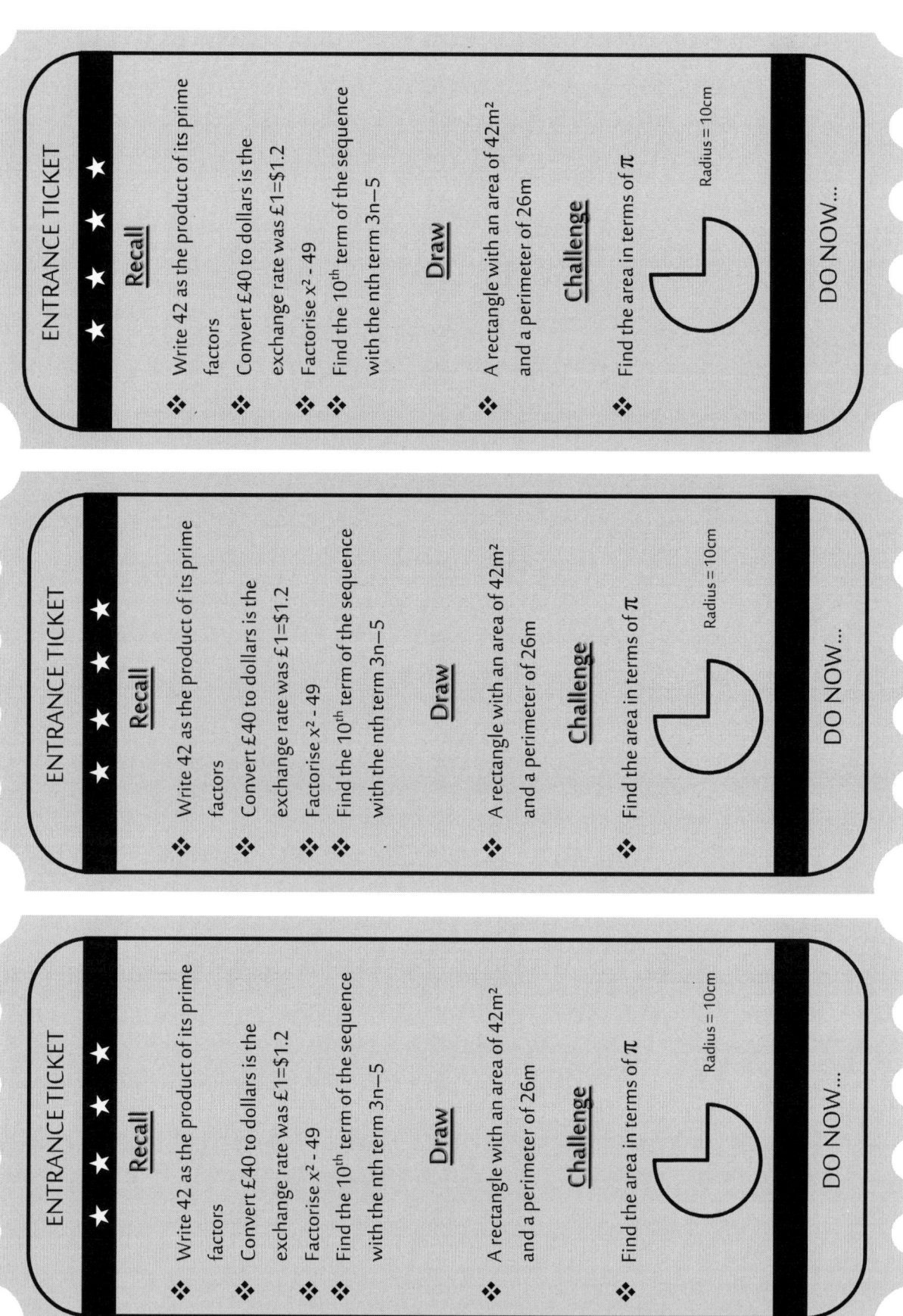

ENTRANCE TICKET ★★★★

Recall

❖ Write 42 as the product of its prime factors

❖ Convert £40 to dollars is the exchange rate was £1=$1.2

❖ Factorise x^2 - 49

❖ Find the 10th term of the sequence with the nth term 3n−5

Draw

❖ A rectangle with an area of $42m^2$ and a perimeter of 26m

Challenge

❖ Find the area in terms of π

Radius = 10cm

DO NOW...

ENTRANCE TICKET ★★★★

Recall

❖ Write 42 as the product of its prime factors

❖ Convert £40 to dollars is the exchange rate was £1=$1.2

❖ Factorise x^2 - 49

❖ Find the 10th term of the sequence with the nth term 3n−5

Draw

❖ A rectangle with an area of $42m^2$ and a perimeter of 26m

Challenge

❖ Find the area in terms of π

Radius = 10cm

DO NOW...

ENTRANCE TICKET ★★★★

Recall

❖ Write 42 as the product of its prime factors

❖ Convert £40 to dollars is the exchange rate was £1=$1.2

❖ Factorise x^2 - 49

❖ Find the 10th term of the sequence with the nth term 3n−5

Draw

❖ A rectangle with an area of $42m^2$ and a perimeter of 26m

Challenge

❖ Find the area in terms of π

Radius = 10cm

DO NOW...

ENTRANCE TICKET ★ ★ ★ ★

Recall

❖ Find 20% Of 160
❖ Expand $(x+3)^2$
❖ Calculate 0.3 x 0.9
❖ Change 0.15 to a percentage
❖ Write the factors of 25
❖ Estimate $\sqrt{99}$
❖ Work out $6.8 \div 4$

Recall

❖ The density formula
❖ The speed formula

Challenge

Estimate

$$\frac{2.3 \times 99.7}{0.5}$$

DO NOW...

ENTRANCE TICKET ★ ★ ★ ★

Recall

❖ Find 20% Of 160
❖ Expand $(x+3)^2$
❖ Calculate 0.3 x 0.9
❖ Change 0.15 to a percentage
❖ Write the factors of 25
❖ Estimate $\sqrt{99}$
❖ Work out $6.8 \div 4$

Recall

❖ The density formula
❖ The speed formula

Challenge

Estimate

$$\frac{2.3 \times 99.7}{0.5}$$

DO NOW...

ENTRANCE TICKET ★ ★ ★ ★

Recall

❖ Find 20% Of 160
❖ Expand $(x+3)^2$
❖ Calculate 0.3 x 0.9
❖ Change 0.15 to a percentage
❖ Write the factors of 25
❖ Estimate $\sqrt{99}$
❖ Work out $6.8 \div 4$

Recall

❖ The density formula
❖ The speed formula

Challenge

Estimate

$$\frac{2.3 \times 99.7}{0.5}$$

DO NOW...

ISBN 978-1-911093-80-0

ENTRANCE TICKET ★ ★ ★ ★

Recall

❖ Calculate 4.5 x 5.4
❖ Factorise 15x − 5
❖ Calculate (-3)²
❖ Solve 5x + 1 > 11
❖ Make x the subject, y = mx + c
❖ Fins 2% of 230
❖ What is the 5th prime number?

Recall

❖ The 3 important rules when completing a bearings question

Challenge

❖ Estimate

$$\frac{1.9 \times 11}{0.2}$$

DO NOW...

ENTRANCE TICKET ★ ★ ★ ★

Recall

❖ Calculate 4.5 x 5.4
❖ Factorise 15x − 5
❖ Calculate (-3)²
❖ Solve 5x + 1 > 11
❖ Make x the subject, y = mx + c
❖ Fins 2% of 230
❖ What is the 5th prime number?

Recall

❖ The 3 important rules when completing a bearings question

Challenge

❖ Estimate

$$\frac{1.9 \times 11}{0.2}$$

DO NOW...

ENTRANCE TICKET ★ ★ ★ ★

Recall

❖ Calculate 4.5 x 5.4
❖ Factorise 15x − 5
❖ Calculate (-3)²
❖ Solve 5x + 1 > 11
❖ Make x the subject, y = mx + c
❖ Fins 2% of 230
❖ What is the 5th prime number?

Recall

❖ The 3 important rules when completing a bearings question

Challenge

❖ Estimate

$$\frac{1.9 \times 11}{0.2}$$

DO NOW...

ENTRANCE TICKET

★ ★ ★ ★

Recall

❖ Simplify 30:5
❖ Expand (x+1)(2x+4)
❖ Calculate 34 x 248
❖ Find the nth term 12, 9, 6...
❖ Work out 34 ÷ 0.5
❖ Solve 5(x-2) = 30
❖ Write 540 as the product of its prime factors

Recall

❖ What the word congruent means

Challenge

❖ Think of a number, multiply by 2, add 5. The answer is 7. What is the number?

DO NOW…

ENTRANCE TICKET

★ ★ ★ ★

Recall

❖ Simplify 30:5
❖ Expand (x+1)(2x+4)
❖ Calculate 34 x 248
❖ Find the nth term 12, 9, 6...
❖ Work out 34 ÷ 0.5
❖ Solve 5(x-2) = 30
❖ Write 540 as the product of its prime factors

Recall

❖ What the word congruent means

Challenge

❖ Think of a number, multiply by 2, add 5. The answer is 7. What is the number?

DO NOW…

ENTRANCE TICKET

★ ★ ★ ★

Recall

❖ Simplify 30:5
❖ Expand (x+1)(2x+4)
❖ Calculate 34 x 248
❖ Find the nth term 12, 9, 6...
❖ Work out 34 ÷ 0.5
❖ Solve 5(x-2) = 30
❖ Write 540 as the product of its prime factors

Recall

❖ What the word congruent means

Challenge

❖ Think of a number, multiply by 2, add 5. The answer is 7. What is the number?

DO NOW…

ENTRANCE TICKET ★ ★ ★ ★

Recall

- ❖ Calculate $30 \div 0.2$
- ❖ Expand $(x+2)(x-7)$
- ❖ Solve $3(x-5) = 30$
- ❖ What is the value of $3x^2$ if $x=4$
- ❖ Find the nth term of the sequence
  4,14,24
- ❖ Calculate 456×3

Sketch

- ❖ A scatter graph with no correlation

Challenge

- ❖ What is the 4th prime number multiplied by the 3rd triangular number?

DO NOW...

ENTRANCE TICKET ★ ★ ★ ★

Recall

- ❖ Calculate $30 \div 0.2$
- ❖ Expand $(x+2)(x-7)$
- ❖ Solve $3(x-5) = 30$
- ❖ What is the value of $3x^2$ if $x=4$
- ❖ Find the nth term of the sequence
  4,14,24
- ❖ Calculate 456×3

Sketch

- ❖ A scatter graph with no correlation

Challenge

- ❖ What is the 4th prime number multiplied by the 3rd triangular number?

DO NOW...

ENTRANCE TICKET ★ ★ ★ ★

Recall

- ❖ Calculate $30 \div 0.2$
- ❖ Expand $(x+2)(x-7)$
- ❖ Solve $3(x-5) = 30$
- ❖ What is the value of $3x^2$ if $x=4$
- ❖ Find the nth term of the sequence
  4,14,24
- ❖ Calculate 456×3

Sketch

- ❖ A scatter graph with no correlation

Challenge

- ❖ What is the 4th prime number multiplied by the 3rd triangular number?

DO NOW...

ENTRANCE TICKET

★ ★ ★ ★

Recall

❖ Work out 3.9 x 0.4
❖ Expand 9x(2x + 3)
❖ Factorise 5x² + 10x
❖ Simplify (2b³)²
❖ What is the 11th term? 6n − 6
❖ Calculate 4 + 2 x 3

Sketch

❖ An acute angle
❖ An obtuse angle
❖ A reflect angle

Challenge

❖ Find x if the perimeter = 62cm

2x + 1

x

DO NOW…

ENTRANCE TICKET

★ ★ ★ ★

Recall

❖ Work out 3.9 x 0.4
❖ Expand 9x(2x + 3)
❖ Factorise 5x² + 10x
❖ Simplify (2b³)²
❖ What is the 11th term? 6n − 6
❖ Calculate 4 + 2 x 3

Sketch

❖ An acute angle
❖ An obtuse angle
❖ A reflect angle

Challenge

❖ Find x if the perimeter = 62cm

2x + 1

x

DO NOW…

ENTRANCE TICKET

★ ★ ★ ★

Recall

❖ Work out 3.9 x 0.4
❖ Expand 9x(2x + 3)
❖ Factorise 5x² + 10x
❖ Simplify (2b³)²
❖ What is the 11th term? 6n − 6
❖ Calculate 4 + 2 x 3

Sketch

❖ An acute angle
❖ An obtuse angle
❖ A reflect angle

Challenge

❖ Find x if the perimeter = 62cm

2x + 1

x

DO NOW…

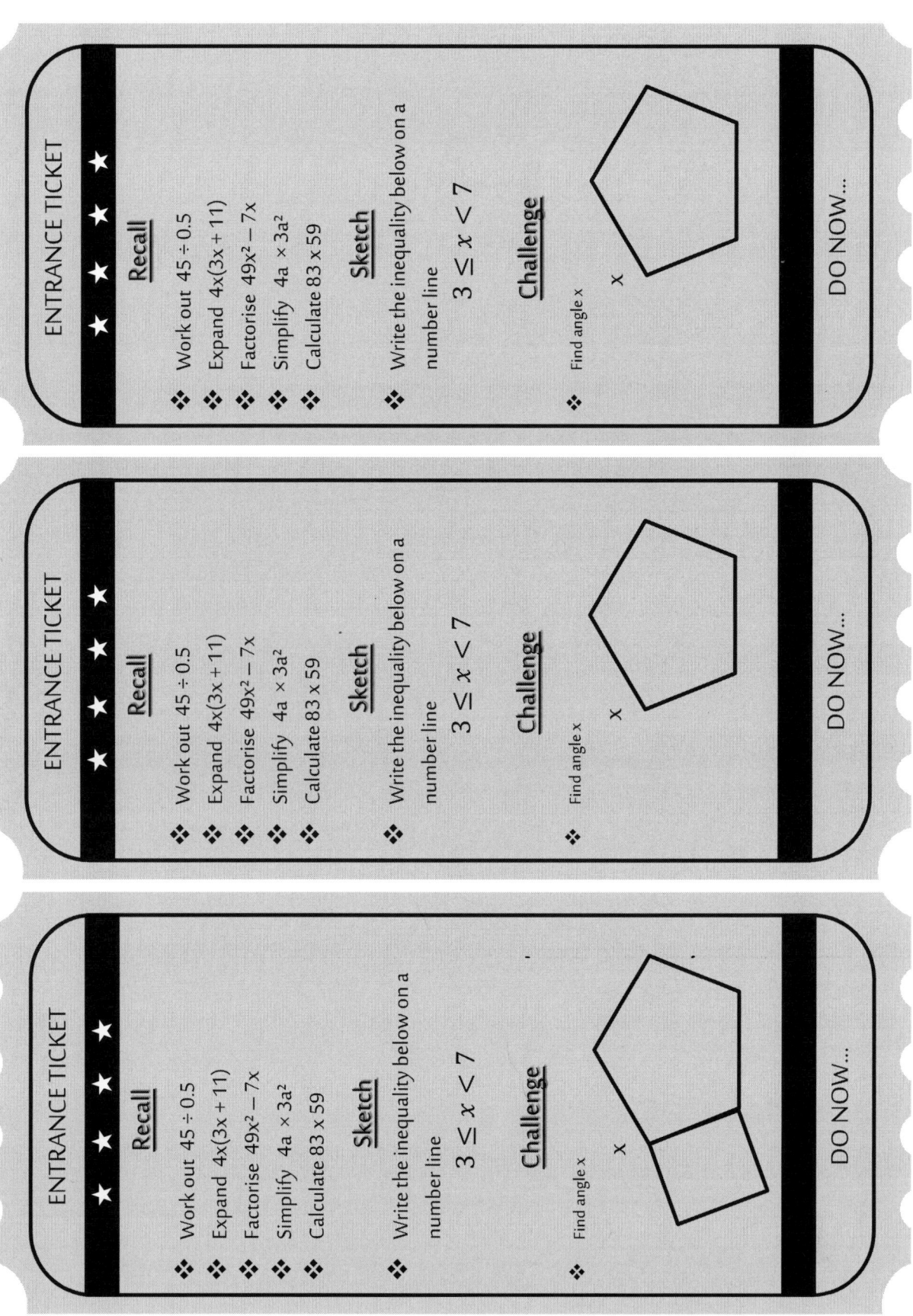

ENTRANCE TICKET ★ ★ ★ ★

Recall

- ❖ Work out $45 \div 0.5$
- ❖ Expand $4x(3x + 11)$
- ❖ Factorise $49x^2 - 7x$
- ❖ Simplify $4a \times 3a^2$
- ❖ Calculate 83×59

Sketch

- ❖ Write the inequality below on a number line

$$3 \leq x < 7$$

Challenge

- ❖ Find angle x

DO NOW...

ENTRANCE TICKET ★ ★ ★ ★

Recall

- ❖ Work out $45 \div 0.5$
- ❖ Expand $4x(3x + 11)$
- ❖ Factorise $49x^2 - 7x$
- ❖ Simplify $4a \times 3a^2$
- ❖ Calculate 83×59

Sketch

- ❖ Write the inequality below on a number line

$$3 \leq x < 7$$

Challenge

- ❖ Find angle x

DO NOW...

ENTRANCE TICKET ★ ★ ★ ★

Recall

- ❖ Work out $45 \div 0.5$
- ❖ Expand $4x(3x + 11)$
- ❖ Factorise $49x^2 - 7x$
- ❖ Simplify $4a \times 3a^2$
- ❖ Calculate 83×59

Sketch

- ❖ Write the inequality below on a number line

$$3 \leq x < 7$$

Challenge

- ❖ Find angle x

DO NOW...

ENTRANCE TICKET ★ ★ ★

Recall

❖ Share £60 in ratio 4:1

❖ Expand (x+3)(2x-5)

❖ Simplify 7 x b x a x 4 x a

❖ Calculate 49 x 23

❖ Write 260 as a product of its prime factors

Sketch

❖ Write the inequality below on a number line

$$5 \leq x < 9$$

Challenge

❖ If the mean = 4, find x

3, 7, 2, 1, x

DO NOW...

ENTRANCE TICKET ★ ★ ★

Recall

❖ Share £60 in ratio 4:1

❖ Expand (x+3)(2x-5)

❖ Simplify 7 x b x a x 4 x a

❖ Calculate 49 x 23

❖ Write 260 as a product of its prime factors

Sketch

❖ Write the inequality below on a number line

$$5 \leq x < 9$$

Challenge

❖ If the mean = 4, find x

3, 7, 2, 1, x

DO NOW...

ENTRANCE TICKET ★ ★ ★

Recall

❖ Share £60 in ratio 4:1

❖ Expand (x+3)(2x-5)

❖ Simplify 7 x b x a x 4 x a

❖ Calculate 49 x 23

❖ Write 260 as a product of its prime factors

Sketch

❖ Write the inequality below on a number line

$$5 \leq x < 9$$

Challenge

❖ If the mean = 4, find x

3, 7, 2, 1, x

DO NOW...

ISBN 978-1-911093-80-0

ENTRANCE TICKET ★ ★ ★ ★

Recall

- ❖ Simplify 4 x b x b x 2 x b
- ❖ Find the nth term of the sequence

  18, 16, 14
- ❖ Expand $4x(5x + 3)$
- ❖ Work out 0.5×0.32
- ❖ Calculate $(2^3-3)^2$

Reasoning

- ❖ Why is 32 not in the sequence with nth term $4n + 2$

Challenge

- ❖ What is the 10th odd number multiplied by the 4th prime number?

DO NOW...

ENTRANCE TICKET ★ ★ ★ ★

Recall

- ❖ Simplify 4 x b x b x 2 x b
- ❖ Find the nth term of the sequence

  18, 16, 14
- ❖ Expand $4x(5x + 3)$
- ❖ Work out 0.5×0.32
- ❖ Calculate $(2^3-3)^2$

Reasoning

- ❖ Why is 32 not in the sequence with nth term $4n + 2$

Challenge

- ❖ What is the 10th odd number multiplied by the 4th prime number?

DO NOW...

ENTRANCE TICKET ★ ★ ★ ★

Recall

- ❖ Simplify 4 x b x b x 2 x b
- ❖ Find the nth term of the sequence

  18, 16, 14
- ❖ Expand $4x(5x + 3)$
- ❖ Work out 0.5×0.32
- ❖ Calculate $(2^3-3)^2$

Reasoning

- ❖ Why is 32 not in the sequence with nth term $4n + 2$

Challenge

- ❖ What is the 10th odd number multiplied by the 4th prime number?

DO NOW...

ENTRANCE TICKET ★ ★ ★ ★

Recall

❖ Write 48 as the product of its prime factors

❖ Convert £36 to dollars is the exchange rate was £1=$1.25

❖ Factorise $x^2 - 100$

❖ Find the 7th term of the sequence with the nth term $3n-12$

Draw

❖ A rectangle with an area of 100m² and a perimeter of 58m

Challenge

❖ Find the area in terms of π

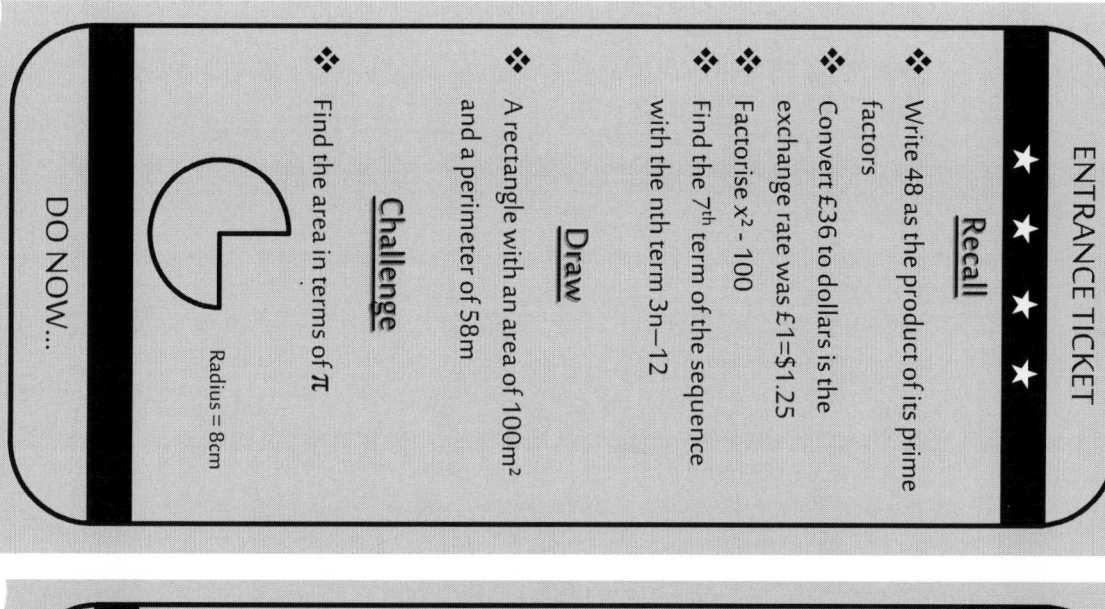

Radius = 8cm

DO NOW...

ENTRANCE TICKET ★ ★ ★ ★

Recall

❖ Write 48 as the product of its prime factors

❖ Convert £36 to dollars is the exchange rate was £1=$1.25

❖ Factorise $x^2 - 100$

❖ Find the 7th term of the sequence with the nth term $3n-12$

Draw

❖ A rectangle with an area of 100m² and a perimeter of 58m

Challenge

❖ Find the area in terms of π

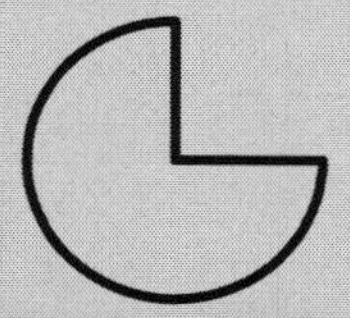

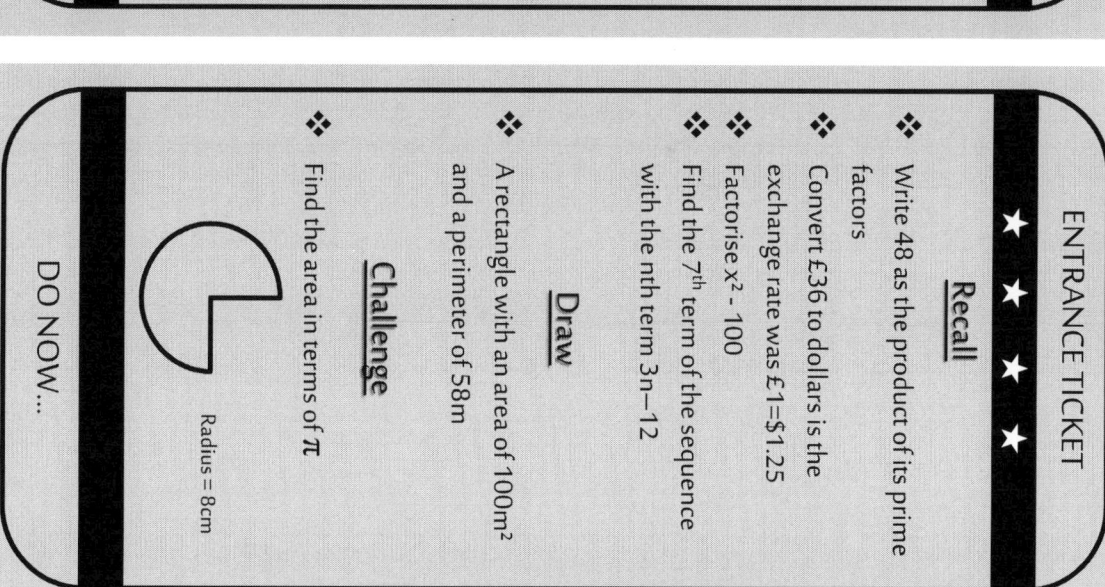

Radius = 8cm

DO NOW...

ENTRANCE TICKET ★ ★ ★ ★

Recall

❖ Write 48 as the product of its prime factors

❖ Convert £36 to dollars is the exchange rate was £1=$1.25

❖ Factorise $x^2 - 100$

❖ Find the 7th term of the sequence with the nth term $3n-12$

Draw

❖ A rectangle with an area of 100m² and a perimeter of 58m

Challenge

❖ Find the area in terms of π

Radius = 8cm

DO NOW...

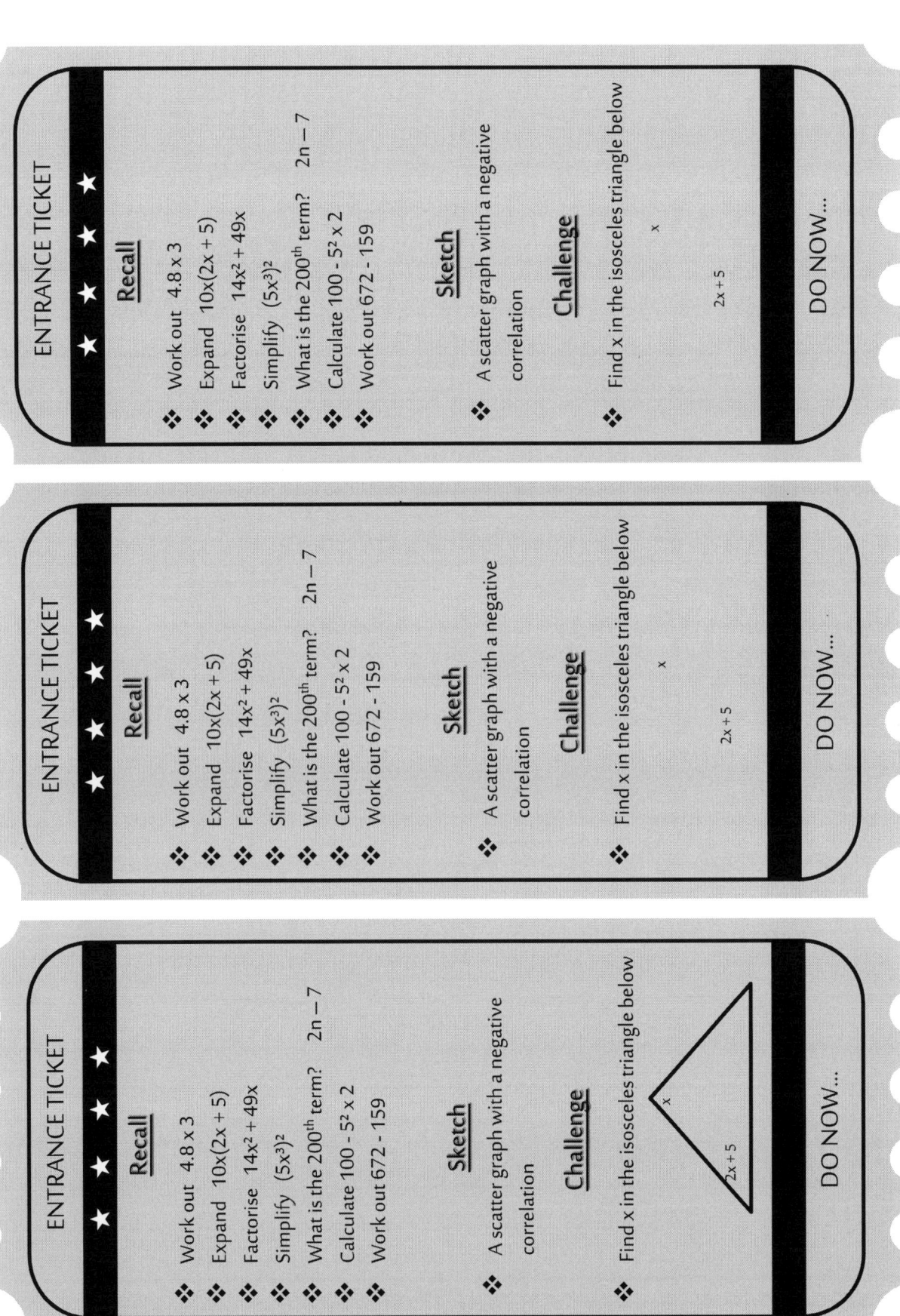

ENTRANCE TICKET ★ ★ ★ ★

Recall

- ❖ Work out 4.8 x 3
- ❖ Expand 10x(2x + 5)
- ❖ Factorise 14x² + 49x
- ❖ Simplify (5x³)²
- ❖ What is the 200th term?   2n − 7
- ❖ Calculate 100 - 5² x 2
- ❖ Work out 672 - 159

Sketch

- ❖ A scatter graph with a negative correlation

Challenge

- ❖ Find x in the isosceles triangle below

x

2x + 5

DO NOW...

ENTRANCE TICKET ★ ★ ★ ★

Recall

- ❖ Work out 4.8 x 3
- ❖ Expand 10x(2x + 5)
- ❖ Factorise 14x² + 49x
- ❖ Simplify (5x³)²
- ❖ What is the 200th term?   2n − 7
- ❖ Calculate 100 - 5² x 2
- ❖ Work out 672 - 159

Sketch

- ❖ A scatter graph with a negative correlation

Challenge

- ❖ Find x in the isosceles triangle below

x

2x + 5

DO NOW...

ENTRANCE TICKET ★ ★ ★ ★

Recall

- ❖ Work out 4.8 x 3
- ❖ Expand 10x(2x + 5)
- ❖ Factorise 14x² + 49x
- ❖ Simplify (5x³)²
- ❖ What is the 200th term?   2n − 7
- ❖ Calculate 100 - 5² x 2
- ❖ Work out 672 - 159

Sketch

- ❖ A scatter graph with a negative correlation

Challenge

- ❖ Find x in the isosceles triangle below

x

2x + 5

DO NOW...

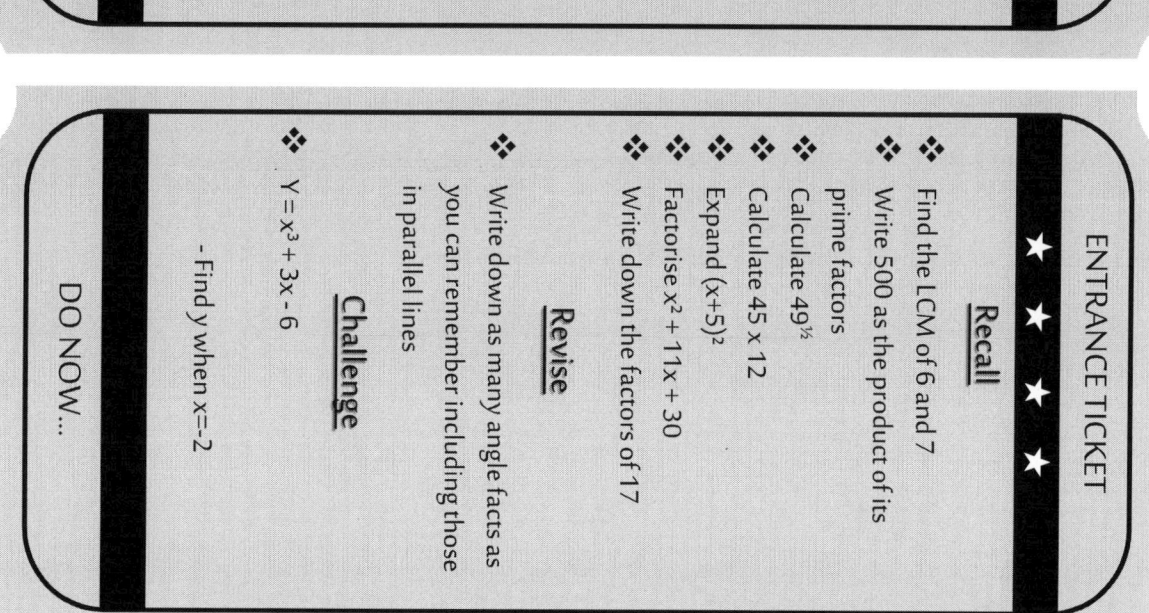

ENTRANCE TICKET ★ ★ ★ ★

Recall

❖ Find the LCM of 6 and 7
❖ Write 500 as the product of its prime factors
❖ Calculate 49½
❖ Calculate 45 x 12
❖ Expand $(x+5)^2$
❖ Factorise $x^2 + 11x + 30$
❖ Write down the factors of 17

Revise

❖ Write down as many angle facts as you can remember including those in parallel lines

Challenge

❖ $Y = x^3 + 3x - 6$

- Find y when x=-2

DO NOW....

ENTRANCE TICKET ★ ★ ★ ★

Recall

❖ Find the LCM of 6 and 7
❖ Write 500 as the product of its prime factors
❖ Calculate 49½
❖ Calculate 45 x 12
❖ Expand $(x+5)^2$
❖ Factorise $x^2 + 11x + 30$
❖ Write down the factors of 17

Revise

❖ Write down as many angle facts as you can remember including those in parallel lines

Challenge

❖ $Y = x^3 + 3x - 6$

- Find y when x=-2

DO NOW....

ENTRANCE TICKET ★ ★ ★ ★

Recall

❖ Find the LCM of 6 and 7
❖ Write 500 as the product of its prime factors
❖ Calculate 49½
❖ Calculate 45 x 12
❖ Expand $(x+5)^2$
❖ Factorise $x^2 + 11x + 30$
❖ Write down the factors of 17

Revise

❖ Write down as many angle facts as you can remember including those in parallel lines

Challenge

❖ $Y = x^3 + 3x - 6$

- Find y when x=-2

DO NOW....

ISBN 978-1-911093-80-0

ENTRANCE TICKET ★ ★ ★ ★

Recall

❖ Calculate $14 \div 0.2$
❖ Expand $(x+2)^2$
❖ Solve $3(x-10) = 30$
❖ Simplify x^0
❖ What is the value of $5x^2$ if $x=2$
❖ Find the nth term of the sequence 14,12,10...
❖ Find the LCM of 4 and 5

Revise

❖ Write an explanation about how you factorise quadratic expression

Challenge

❖ $Y = x^3 + 2x + 8$
  - Find y when $x=-2$

DO NOW...

ENTRANCE TICKET ★ ★ ★ ★

Recall

❖ Calculate $14 \div 0.2$
❖ Expand $(x+2)^2$
❖ Solve $3(x-10) = 30$
❖ Simplify x^0
❖ What is the value of $5x^2$ if $x=2$
❖ Find the nth term of the sequence 14,12,10...
❖ Find the LCM of 4 and 5

Revise

❖ Write an explanation about how you factorise quadratic expression

Challenge

❖ $Y = x^3 + 2x + 8$
  - Find y when $x=-2$

DO NOW...

ENTRANCE TICKET ★ ★ ★ ★

Recall

❖ Calculate $14 \div 0.2$
❖ Expand $(x+2)^2$
❖ Solve $3(x-10) = 30$
❖ Simplify x^0
❖ What is the value of $5x^2$ if $x=2$
❖ Find the nth term of the sequence 14,12,10...
❖ Find the LCM of 4 and 5

Revise

❖ Write an explanation about how you factorise quadratic expression

Challenge

❖ $Y = x^3 + 2x + 8$
  - Find y when $x=-2$

DO NOW...

ISBN 978-1-911093-80-0

ENTRANCE TICKET ★ ★ ★

Recall

❖ Find 23% of 480

❖ Simplify b x b x b x b

❖ Work out the sum of 2^4 and 4^3

❖ Write as an inequality,   x is greater than 7

❖ Write 18 as a percentage of 27

True or False?

❖ $\dfrac{7}{20}$ is in between...... $\dfrac{3}{4}$ and $\dfrac{4}{5}$

Calculator skills

❖ Calculate $\dfrac{17.4 + 3.9}{1.3 + 0.8}$

DO NOW...

ENTRANCE TICKET ★ ★ ★

Recall

❖ Find 23% of 480

❖ Simplify b x b x b x b

❖ Work out the sum of 2^4 and 4^3

❖ Write as an inequality,   x is greater than 7

❖ Write 18 as a percentage of 27

True or False?

❖ $\dfrac{7}{20}$ is in between...... $\dfrac{3}{4}$ and $\dfrac{4}{5}$

Calculator skills

❖ Calculate $\dfrac{17.4 + 3.9}{1.3 + 0.8}$

DO NOW...

ENTRANCE TICKET ★ ★ ★

Recall

❖ Find 23% of 480

❖ Simplify b x b x b x b

❖ Work out the sum of 2^4 and 4^3

❖ Write as an inequality,   x is greater than 7

❖ Write 18 as a percentage of 27

True or False?

❖ $\dfrac{7}{20}$ is in between...... $\dfrac{3}{4}$ and $\dfrac{4}{5}$

Calculator skills

❖ Calculate $\dfrac{17.4 + 3.9}{1.3 + 0.8}$

DO NOW...

ENTRANCE TICKET

Recall

❖ Find the nth term of the sequence -

2, 4, 10, 16

❖ Work out 1820 ÷ 28

❖ Write 4/5 as a percentage

❖ Write in standard form 0.00734

❖ Simplify $16x^8 \div 8x^4$

True or False?

❖ The range of the following

numbers is -19

-20, -10, -6, -1

Calculator skills

❖ Calculate $\dfrac{(4.63)^2}{5.1}$

DO NOW...

ENTRANCE TICKET

Recall

❖ Find the nth term of the sequence -

2, 4, 10, 16

❖ Work out 1820 ÷ 28

❖ Write 4/5 as a percentage

❖ Write in standard form 0.00734

❖ Simplify $16x^8 \div 8x^4$

True or False?

❖ The range of the following

numbers is -19

-20, -10, -6, -1

Calculator skills

❖ Calculate $\dfrac{(4.63)^2}{5.1}$

DO NOW...

ENTRANCE TICKET

Recall

❖ Find the nth term of the sequence -

2, 4, 10, 16

❖ Work out 1820 ÷ 28

❖ Write 4/5 as a percentage

❖ Write in standard form 0.00734

❖ Simplify $16x^8 \div 8x^4$

True or False?

❖ The range of the following

numbers is -19

-20, -10, -6, -1

Calculator skills

❖ Calculate $\dfrac{(4.63)^2}{5.1}$

DO NOW...

ENTRANCE TICKET ★ ★ ★ ★

Recall

❖ Work out 52 x 21
❖ Write 280 as the product of its prime factors
❖ Calculate 4/5 of 60
❖ Make y the subject   x = 3y
  + 8
❖ Calculate 6 x 3² - 7
❖ Expand 2a(3b + 7)
❖ Work out 2.3 x 1.8

True or False?

❖ 2600ml is greater that 2.6l

Calculator skills

❖ Calculate
$$\frac{\sqrt{7.93}}{3.14 + 4.16}$$

DO NOW...

ENTRANCE TICKET ★ ★ ★ ★

Recall

❖ Work out 52 x 21
❖ Write 280 as the product of its prime factors
❖ Calculate 4/5 of 60
❖ Make y the subject   x = 3y
  + 8
❖ Calculate 6 x 3² - 7
❖ Expand 2a(3b + 7)
❖ Work out 2.3 x 1.8

True or False?

❖ 2600ml is greater that 2.6l

Calculator skills

❖ Calculate
$$\frac{\sqrt{7.93}}{3.14 + 4.16}$$

DO NOW...

ENTRANCE TICKET ★ ★ ★ ★

Recall

❖ Work out 52 x 21
❖ Write 280 as the product of its prime factors
❖ Calculate 4/5 of 60
❖ Make y the subject   x = 3y
  + 8
❖ Calculate 6 x 3² - 7
❖ Expand 2a(3b + 7)
❖ Work out 2.3 x 1.8

True or False?

❖ 2600ml is greater that 2.6l

Calculator skills

❖ Calculate
$$\frac{\sqrt{7.93}}{3.14 + 4.16}$$

DO NOW...

ISBN 978-1-911093-80-0

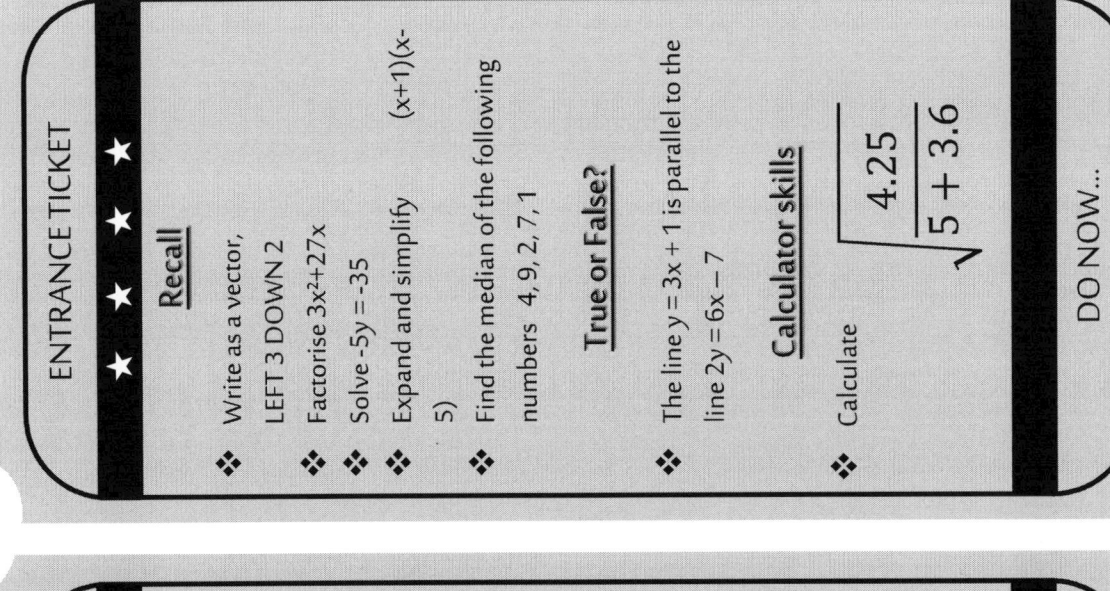

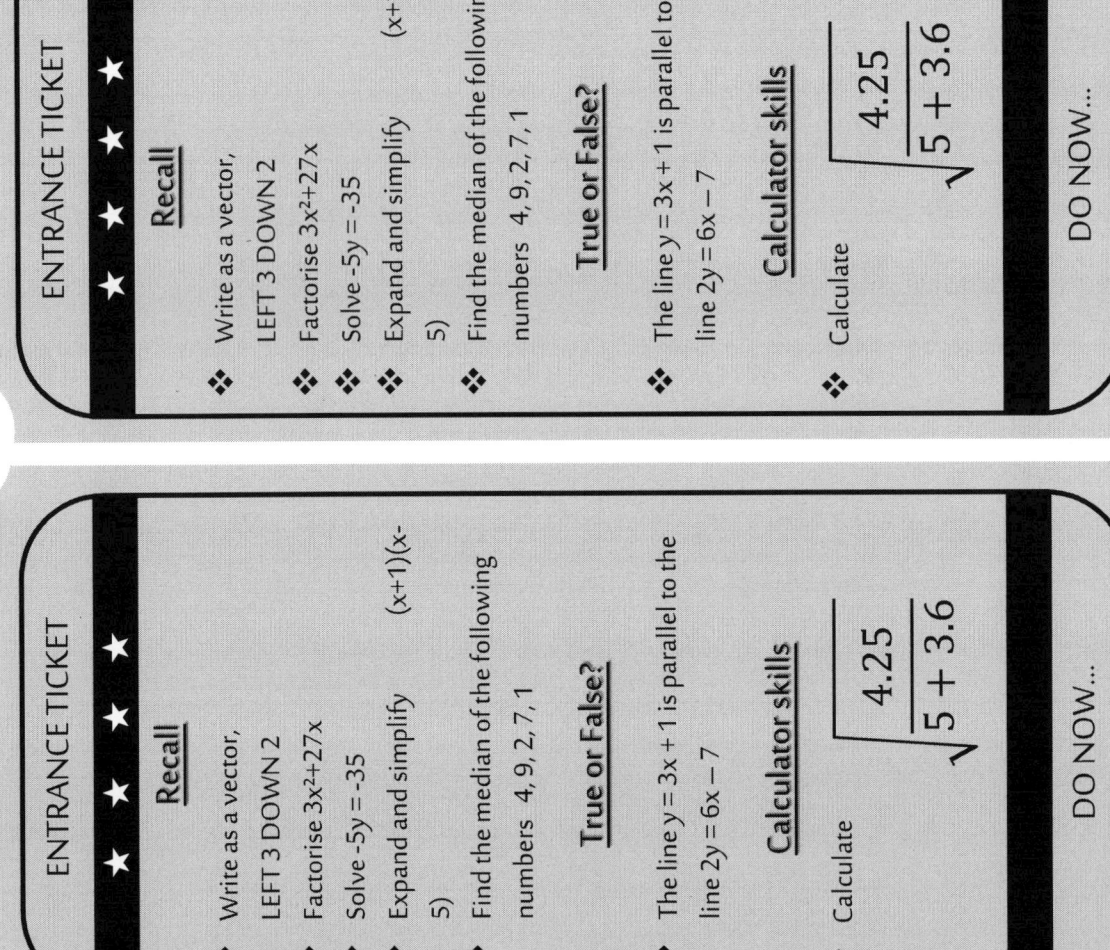

The three tickets each read:

ENTRANCE TICKET

Recall

❖ Write as a vector, LEFT 3 DOWN 2

❖ Factorise $3x^2 + 27x$

❖ Solve $-5y = -35$

❖ Expand and simplify $(x+1)(x-5)$

❖ Find the median of the following numbers 4, 9, 2, 7, 1

True or False?

❖ The line $y = 3x + 1$ is parallel to the line $2y = 6x - 7$

Calculator skills

❖ Calculate $\sqrt{\dfrac{4.25}{5 + 3.6}}$

DO NOW...

Answers

1)	2)	3)
100	0.06	90
$x^2+11x+28$	$12x^2+15x$	$15x^2-30x$
3	$3x(x+2)$	$7(7x-1)$
50	a^6	$12a^3$
$-2n+12$	33	1127
Sketch	Sketch – two sides the same	Sketch x 2
88	e.g. rectangle	108
	X=5	

4)	5)	6)
240:60	$15b^2$	240:300:60
x^2-x-20	$2n+2$	$x^2-4x-12$
$6a^2b$	$20x-32$	A
3285	0.01	56
2^5 X 5	206	2^3x3x5
Equally likely	Sketch x 2	5 x 6
X=6	117	X=8

ISBN 978-1-911093-80-0

Answers

7)
160
$8x^2-28x$
$(x+2)(x+3)$
$16a^2$
6
1768
50
120

8)
$2 \times 3 \times 7$
$48
$(x+7)(x-7)$
25
6x7
75π

9)
32
x^2+6x+9
0.27
15%
1,5,15
10
1.7
Density=mass/volume
Speed = distance/time

10)
24.3
$5(3x-1)$
9
$X=2$
$X = (y-c)/m$
4.6
11
Start from north, clockwise, 3 figures
100

11)
6:1
$2x^2+6x+4$
8680
$-3n+15$
68
$X=8$
$2^2 \times 3^3 \times 5$
Same dimensions
$X=1$

12)
150
$x^2-5x-14$
$X=15$
48
$10n-6$
1368
Sketch
42

ISBN 978-1-911093-80-0

Answers

13)
1.56
$18x^2+27x$
$5x(x+2)$
$4b^6$
60
10
Sketches
10

14)
90
$12x^2+44x$
$7x(7x-1)$
$12a^3$
4897

3   7

162

15)
48:12
$2x^2+x-15$
$28a^2b$
1127
$2^2 \times 5 \times 13$

5   9

7

16)
$8b^3$
-2n+20
$20x^2+12x$
0.16
25
Between 8th and 9th term
140

17)
$2^4 \times 3$
45
(x+10)(x-10)
9
25x4
48π

18)
14.4
$20x^2+50x$
$7x(2x+7)$
$25x^6$
393
50
513
Sketch
34

ISBN 978-1-911093-80-0

Answers

19)
42
$2^2 \times 5^3$
7
540
$x^2+10x+25$
$(x+5)(x+6)$
1 and 17
Angle facts
-20

20)
70
x^2+4x+4
20
1
20
-2n+16
20
Explanation
-4

21)
110.4
b^4
80
$x > 7$
66.7%
False as over 16/20
10.1428571

22)
$6n - 8$
65
16%
7.34×10^{-3}
$2x^4$
False 19
4.20331373

23)
1092
$2^3 \times 5 \times 7$
48
$y = (x - 8)/3$
47
$6ab + 14a$
4.14
False the same
0.385756927

24)
$\begin{pmatrix} -3 \\ -2 \end{pmatrix}$
$3x(x+9)$
$y = 7$
x^2-4x-5
4
True same gradient 3
0.702983674

Printed and bound by CPI Group (UK) Ltd, Croydon, CR0 4YY

23/02/2026

02058825-0003